My Mother Taught Me

A collection of prose, poetry, and photography celebrating maternal lessons that have shaped our current selves

Edited by Sueann Wells

Dedication

Naturally, this book is dedicated to our collective Mothers, without whom none of us would be who we are today.

The editor would also like to thank all the children who take time to cherish the mothers and mother figures in their lives. Life can be crazy, and Life does not slow down for any of us. We need to search within our souls to recognize the power of our maternal lessons and to pay proper tribute to those who came before us, paving the way for our current lives. May we pay it forward, making each generation's lives better on our quest to be the best humans we can be.

ISBN: 978-1-365-78785-0
Copyright 2017 Sueann Wells
            Mother Muse Publishing

No part of this publication may be reproduced, distributed, or transmitted in any form or by any means, including photocopying, recording, or other electronic or mechanical methods, without the prior permission of the publisher, except in the case of brief quotations embodied in critical reviews and certain other noncommercial uses permitted by copyright law.

For reprint permission, to arrange readings, or to order copies with a bulk discount, contact the editor directly at RochesterNYEditor@yahoo.com.

motherly-musings.com

CONTENTS

Editor's Note 6

Mom Taught Me that Family Matters 7

    The real thing   8
        ~ Jerri Lynn Sparks
    Walk in the woods   10
        ~ Sueann Wells
    Mom's report card   13
        ~ Emery L. Campbell
    Forgiveness, glitter and milkshakes   15
        ~ Jerri Lynn Sparks
    Ma's geometry   19
        ~ Ron Bailey
    Education through silent example   20
        ~ Cyndalynn Tilley
    College break flu   23
        ~ Ron Bailey
    Ma   24
        ~ Ron Bailey
    Love is the only thing you need   26
        ~ Katelynn Vukosic
    To the moon and back   26
        ~ Kay Vukosic

Mom Taught Me to Be Responsible 27

    Always turn the light off   28
        ~ Krista Gleason
    Live within your means and you will have the
        means to live   30
        ~ Karen Hockenberry
    The list   34
        ~ Susan Baruch

Ma was a counter 38
~ *Ron Bailey*
Mothers know best (sometimes) 39
~ *Karen Hockenberry*
Oops! 41
~ *Kayla Wells*
All opinions matter ~ Let your voice be heard 43
~ *Sueann Wells*
Work hard 48
~ *Karen Hockenberry*

Mom Taught Me to Be the Best I Can Be 50

Finding a good melon 51
~ *Jerri Lynn Sparks*
Like mother, like daughter 55
~ *Karla Linn Merrifield*
Change a bad system from within 57
~ *Karen Hockenberry*
Take time to rest 59
~ *Sueann Wells*
Taking a vacation from me 64
~ *Sue Vogt*
Wise words 69
~ *Heidi Banser*
Mother Eva 70
~ *Holly Strickland*

Mom had her Faults, as All Humans Do, but Because of these faults I am Me 73

"Put a Band-Aid on it" and other lessons learned
from my mother 74
~ *Laila Suleiman Dahan*
No forth 80
~ *Karla Linn Merrifield*

Lesson	82
~ *M.J. Iuppa*	
Moms are human, too	83
~ *Karen Hockenberry*	

Contributors' Index **80**

Note from the Editor's Desk

This is the year for peace, making peace with our selves and our neighbors, cherishing those closest to us, appreciating differences between us as humans, and mending fences broken by disagreement or discord. It is never too late to reconcile or to make a concerted effort toward peace, love, and understanding.

To best understand ourselves, we need to understand our heritage. We must look inward, make peace within our own souls, and recognize those who have shaped our beings. We all have mothers who have impacted who we are today. We must learn from and grow with the lessons they have shown us.

In this volume you will find inspirational pieces by writers and photographers who seek to celebrate these formative lessons. No matter what kind of relationship you have with your own mother, you must understand your past to make your future great. Make time for a better you. Reflect. Hopefully, you will find inspiration within this volume.

Thank you to all the great contributors who have made this project an enjoyable work of heart again for me. I cherish the opportunity to work with writers and photographers to make our slice of life more positive and inspirational. Life is challenging. Let's celebrate the positive, and learn from the good and the bad.

Thank you, readers, for the opportunity to share these great works with the world. May the Mother Muse inspire you to be the best human you possibly can be. If we all seek love, peace, and understanding, this globe we share will shine. Let's make our legacy a great one!

Cordially,

Sueann Wells

Mom Taught Me that Family Matters

The real thing

We never had artificial sweeteners in our house growing up
My mother would never allow it
Instead of diet soda swirling around in my cup
we had the real thing and that was about it

We had sugar, maple syrup, molasses and honey
The only sweet and low we had was music on the radio
We were always running short on gas and money
but we were rich with life lessons on which way to go

We didn't drink water unless it was from the hose
and we certainly didn't sip on herbal tea
We didn't wear fancy designer clothes
to church where we confessed for eternity

Our biscuits were homemade and dripping with butter
The word "Lite" did not enter through our country door
We had the full-on life and all its clutter
with salt, laughter and screams, and always room for more

If we had a party, it was for the whole neighborhood
and everyone brought an ingredient or two to share
We'd sit outside until the sleepy sun rose for good
eating sausages and eggs and lounging in the country air

And if we were sick with a fever or sore throat
my mother would make medicine on the stove
She cooked it up from recipes she never wrote
but which were handed down as a family treasure trove

There were no trips to the nurse or the doctor
unless someone had an obviously broken bone
My mother or grandmother would be the medical proctor
They never called the hospital on the phone

Maybe it was borne out of economic strife
but I think a lot of it was about caring for your own
We tend to contract out way too much of life
instead of nurturing love within our own home

My mother taught me that life is to be lived with verve:
To wear the glitter, eat the cake, tell the boy you love him
If danger comes your way always be ready to swerve
and to trust in God and never put anyone above Him

And now that I'm raising a family of my own
The real thing pervades our home life too
There's sugar and honey in our sweet little home
because Mama taught me nothing artificial will do

Jerri Lynn Sparks

Jerri Lynn Sparks is a single mother of four, two of whom are now grown and out of the house. Originally from North Carolina, Sparks has lived in Rochester, NY for the past fifteen years. A former Congressional Press Secretary, she has written political editorials, press releases, legislative texts and campaign materials in addition to poetry and essays on life and love. Her work has been featured in Germ Magazine, *the* Democrat & Chronicle, *the* Kinston Free Press, *and in a previous anthology of* Motherly Musings. *Her day job is as Director of Global Logistics for a pharmaceutical research lab, a job she loves because it combines the creativity of persuasive communication with her research degree from UCLA while also improving world health. In her free time, Sparks loves to be outside running, hiking and working in her garden. On Sundays she bakes and writes. A Southerner by birth, she has come to call the North (aka "the tundra," as she jokingly refers to it) her adoptive home.*

Walk in the Woods

Unable to silence my heavy winter boot-laden steps, I look out upon the snowy forest scape and think of my mother. At my childhood home we would often go for family walks down our rural county road ... Ben and I would often plead the case for skipping this outing, and sometimes these nice family walks started off as icy adventures even in the middle of summer.

As preteens, Ben and I thought we could affect change simply by acting grumpy and not participating in the conversation. Harumphing and stomping or kicking up the gravel on the road's shoulder, keeping our eyes on our feet, ignoring questions from our parents, maybe shrugging our cold shoulders in response to loving parental questions. That sort of passive-aggression. It works, right? Silly preteens. Mom and Dad saw through that.

It didn't last long, though, and once we were only a few minutes down the road, something in our parent's conversation, or something around us, or some thought that popped into our heads would pull us out of our funk. We would quit our kibitzing, as mom would say, and we'd join in the conversation. I remember one time my particularly grumpy self did a full 180 and literally skipped down the road telling my parents some jewel of information about my school day or week. Those knowing parental prying questions loosened the noose on my angst, and I rejoined the family.

Sometimes, when Ben and I were particularly disgruntled at being forced to go for a walk, the wayward, crazy drivers along our busy road would break the icy silence and we'd all come together heading farther off the shoulder, my dad or mom gesturing at the unaware drivers, yelling "SLOW DOWN! It's 55 here!" like the drivers were cognizant enough to hear them and register what they said. It would break the ice nicely, though, and one of us kids would cross over to the light side, and one grump against three didn't stand a chance, so we'd all end up pleasant with each other and with the world again.

I cherished those walks as a family, spending a few minutes simply being together, with no housework, no schoolwork, no arguments, just chatting and getting some exercise together. Now that I am a mother and my little ones are not so little anymore, I want that for my own nuclear family too. It's often a huge ordeal to get one or another of my daughters to stop what she is doing to go for a walk. My husband and I often will give advance notice, work out a compromise with the girls who are deep in play, all the tricks of the good parenthood trade, and still there are battles just to get outside together.

"I just don't want to go in the woods," my middle child will often whine. We live just outside a huge county park so we get to enjoy the beauty of the park as well as the joy of family togetherness. Win-win. We don't have to worry about wayward traffic, and we get to see lots of wildlife – right in our own backyard. No grump stands a chance here.

Once we are out in the woods, the girls will often embark on fantastical adventures full of witches and goblins, excitement and peril, using fallen logs and animal tracks as catalysts for some sort of new twist in their play. Truly, we get only about half a mile into the walk each time before all the girls are bubbly and happy again that we are out in the woods. Hubby and I will catch up on the latest news and gossip we miss in the daily parenting routine and discuss whatever matters are pressing at the moment. And we all return home happy and delighted we went for a walk in the woods after all … even the naysayer daughter, or the grumpy, sometimes-angst-filled mini-me preteen.

My mom must have stressed so much over my brother and I being so grumpy starting off on those walks back then. Or thought her daughter was the bitchiest girl on the planet. (Sorry, Mom!) But I am so glad they 'forced' us to go for walks as a family. In the whirlwind of life, it was simply divine to stop, get out of our own little worlds for a few minutes, and spend quality time together. I look forward to many walks together as a family as my own children grow into beautiful human beings!

Sueann Wells

Momma taught me to appreciate nature ~ This is one of my favorite paths in Mendon Ponds Park.
Sueann Wells

Mom's Report Card

Her mother's driving Margaret, seven, to
a girl friend's house to play when Meg says, "Mom,
how old are you?" "Good gracious Meggie, you
should never ask a lady that," she calm-

ly answers. "Why?" "Because it's not polite."
"OK." A pause, then "How much do you weigh?"
"Now really," says her mother, "you've no right
to pry. What has come over you today?"

Undaunted, Meg persists. "I'd like to know
why you and Daddy got divorced." "Now that's
enough, my girl. It's time for you to go
and play." The mother stops the car and pats

her daughter on the head and waves goodbye.
"My mom won't tell me anything," says Meggie to her friend. "It does no good to cry
about it," says the girl, "and don't try beg-

"ging. Listen, what you have to do is this:
just take a careful look at—what's it called?--
oh yeah, her drivers license. You can't miss.
It's like the card from school. It tells it all.

"It's full of lots of private stuff you need."
That night when she's back home our little Meggie steals a peek in Mommie's purse to read
her license. In the morning over egg

and toast she says to Mother, "Now it's clear
to me how old you are. You're thirty-three."
"However did you find that out, my dear?"
asks Mom. But Meg keeps on, "And now you see,

I know your weight: one hundred twenty pounds."
Her mom's agape. "How in the world…? I'm vexed
with you." But Meg insists. "And I have found
why you divorced. You got an F in sex."

Emery L. Campbell

Emery L. Campbell is an award-winning writer. He has two published books of poetry: This Gardener's Impossible Dream: A Not So Green Thumb (or Why I Took Up Poetry Instead) *(2005, Multicultural Press), and* Selected Fables and Poems in Translation *(2010, Print1Direct). Email the poet at <u>elcampbell08@comcast.net</u>. Campbell's works have appeared in many journals, anthologies, magazines and newsletters over the years. His work has won awards from the National Federation of State Poetry Societies, the Georgia Writers Association, the Georgia Poetry Society, and other individual state poetry organizations. Campbell has twice been awarded the title of U. S. National Senior Poet Laureate for poets over the age of fifty. Campbell's pre-poet days were spent as a U.S. naval aviator, post-graduate student in France, and an export sales executive with ITT Rayonier, Inc. Campbell has traveled widely for business and pleasure. He and his wife, Hettie, now live in Lawrenceville, GA. The couple has an adult son, Lucas, who resides in suburban Atlanta.*

Forgiveness, glitter and milkshakes

My momma taught me that life should come with forgiveness, glitter and milkshakes. Allow me to explain…

I'm sitting here by my kitchen window anxiously waiting for my teenaged daughter to bring my car back from her very first solo drive and my mind goes where every parent's mind goes:

It's been ten minutes; is she in a ditch?
Did she crash into another car?
Did she hit a tree or a deer or a pedestrian?
Oh GOD, did she crash into a *store*?

While I'm going through my internal parental panic list, I recall all the times I did the same thing to my own mother.

Once, when I was just learning to drive, I drove us both, along with my best friend who was between us in the front seat, straight into a cow pasture. Apparently my scrawny teenaged arms weren't strong enough to handle the wheel without power steering. The cows were intrigued; my mother was not. However, I don't remember getting into much trouble that day other than having to listen to my best friend describe The Great Cow Pasture Adventure to all our friends at school the next day.

My mom made me get back in the car and keep on driving, day after day until I learned to exist out in the world by myself.

Another time, senior prom night to be exact, I was so late and so scared to go back home (*because* I was so late), that I decided to just not go home. In teenage logic this made perfect sense. Because my date had been a jerk, I had gone to my cousin's house to take a nap and cried myself to sleep, waking up around 3 a.m. By then I was petrified, and my cousin and I decided the best thing to do was continue sleeping and work it out in the morning. Big mistake. Teenage logic should be outlawed.

Not being a parent yet, I had no idea what I was doing to my poor mother and father. They were up all night worried that I:

Was in a ditch,
Crashed into another car,
Hit a tree or a deer or a pedestrian, or
Crashed into a *store*.

This was before cell phones and Facebook so there was no way to track me or contact me. They barely knew my date, a co-worker at my new job (also BIG mistake), so they basically called *everyone* I'd ever known so the entire countryside was looking for me and spreading the word of this horrible thing I had supposedly done.

By 7 a.m. my parents had figured out where I was and rang my cousin's house. He answered the phone and ran into the room where I was sleeping and hastily woke me up. I don't recall what my parents said other than "You'd better get home NOW!"

So my poor cousin had the awful task of racing me home and simultaneously avoiding my furious parents. The moment his car pulled into my driveway, I got out and my cousin barreled out of there as fast as he could. I can still see it in my mind, like he was in the Dukes of Hazzard racing out of there.

Now I had to face them all alone: the World's Angriest Parents. It was so much worse than I thought.

When I stepped through the door, prom dress all wrinkled, hair and makeup a mess from crying over my lousy prom date, a guy I'd been crushing on for months and who had turned out to be the worst date ever, there sat not only my parents but many of my aunts and uncles as well. This was *horrifying*. It was as if I was facing a military crimes tribunal with no lawyer and no preparation, and the generals were my parents. I was going to get shellacked!

"Where have you been, young lady?" my mother demanded, but before I could even speak, my dad, who had so much anger on his face I thought he was going to explode, jumped in accusing me of being out all night with "that boy." I tried to assure him nothing had happened but my words fell on the deafest ears EVER.

Finally, after what seemed like an hour, my mother was satisfied and sent everyone home. She stood up to my dad and called his crazy off. She had her girl back home safe and sound. Exhausted and emotionally drained, she looked at me in the early morning light, the remnants of what should have been a magical night barely hanging onto me, and said, "Go on to bed now and get some sleep. Don't EVER do that to me again, do you hear me? Do you know what ran through my mind all night? Don't you ever do that again."

And I never did. I always called after that. No matter how bad it was or how late it was, I always called.

After that it became a joke in my family that I still haven't come home from my senior prom. Somehow we turned my parents' worst nightmare into a running family joke (one that my dad still doesn't laugh over, by the way).

Later that day, my mom and I went out for burgers, fries and milkshakes to ease the tension in the house. I didn't even bother wiping off the prom night glitter, preferring instead to wear my sparkly battle scars like a defeated princess. We bonded over the ineptitude of a certain type of boy and it was a revelation to me that she even *had* experience with the sort. It made me feel like, despite our differences, we were in the same tribe, my mother and me. And she protected me from my dad's wrath that day, and I'll never forget that.

All these years later, I guess I'd say that what my momma taught me is that as long as your babies are safe and sound, take it as a gift and don't question it too much. She always used to say, "Don't look a gift horse in the mouth." Somehow, you dig down deep into yourself and find forgiveness. You see the glitter on your child and know that it represents the hope for better things and you mourn with her when the glitter's promise doesn't materialize. And, more importantly, you buy her more glitter along with big, thick, chocolate milkshakes the morning after heartbreak so she learns how to exist out in the world all by herself.

So yeah, my momma taught me life should come with forgiveness, glitter and milkshakes.

Jerri Lynn Sparks

Teaching Jared to Shave
Jerri Lynn Sparks

ma's geometry

          grandwomen knit quilts
       watch every stitch
     see their image and mine in tight dna threads
       cut from a pattern generations old
each square precise
    knobby fingers dry and parched
  hold edges
      fringes and needles

some squares fit oddly
      in perfect imperfection

a pandemonium of color blends
in tiny scuttles
    fabrics fray and weaken
    each is part of a family quilt
     ma hangs on the wall

  look at its symmetry from across the room
boxed in edges of doorframe
        walk closer
see where blue perspired on yellow thread
                        green
   a patch from ma's christmas apron
cranberry stain still there
    crooked quilt
    another odd brick in her family portrait

Ron Bailey

Education through silent example

My dad died when I was 14. I was a daddy's girl. I loved being with him. He'd take me on motorcycle rides and depending on the weather, we'd stop for hot chocolate or ice cream. I used to pretend to be asleep when we came home late at night, so he'd carry me in the house. We had big plans. I was going to get my toe shoes and be a ballet dancer. He loved me, supported me and enjoyed seeing me dance around the house.

I remember that September day. I knew something was wrong when I saw my mom's reddened eyes. She was a strong woman. I don't remember ever seeing her cry before. Somehow, I knew before she said it that my dad was gone. They had a good marriage. My dad was a pleasant, helpful and kind husband. He loved her and treated her like the precious gem she was.

All of that was then gone. My life changed. I was heart-broken. I never considered the effect on my mom. She acted strong. She didn't complain. She did what she had to do. We rarely saw eye-to-eye. We routinely had disagreements. I remember overhearing my aunt tell her what a brat I was. Mom didn't agree. She understood my struggles. I never understood hers. I probably still don't.

Despite all that, I knew my mom loved me. She showed her love by massaging my temples whenever I had a migraine. She could see in my eyes when I didn't feel well. She did the best she could. I learned valuable lessons from her.

One day I was so mad at my sister; we were egging each other on. In those days, we had our milk delivered and I was supposed to put the empty milk jug out on the porch for pick up, but I was mad and out of control. Instead of placing it on the porch, I threw that milk jug at my sister with all the strength I had. I guess I was pretty strong, but alas, a bad aim. That milk jug flew past my sister and shattered the window. I thought, 'My mom is going to kill me. I am in so much trouble.'

But that's not the only window I broke. One day, I was locked out of the house and I broke the basement window trying to break in. Another time, I knocked over a carnival glass plate my mom inherited from her mom. Once, I put a hot curling iron on a chair and burned it. That chair is now mine and still has the burn mark.

Each time, I knew I was in trouble. Mom didn't yell or get mad; she simply took care of it. My mom's silence taught me that people, me in particular, are more important than material things. My mom taught me what really matters.

Back in the 1980s when my dad died, organ donation wasn't discussed much. There was no campaign educating people about it. There was no organ donation box on a driver's license. We weren't prepared for the question. 'Would you like to donate your husband's organs?' Say What?! My dad had barely died and they were begging us for his organs! They wanted to cut him up and give his parts away. I couldn't believe they asked. But my mom said, 'Yes.' She knew and taught me by example that no matter what tragedy is going on in my own life, I can help and serve others.

My mom struggled to support us financially. It's hard being a single mom. She supported two children away in Europe and three at home. She took care of our basic needs and so much more. My mom found a way to feed, clothe and house us. It wasn't easy, and yes, we got help from our church, but she did it. She would take us to the food pantry to work and show our gratitude for the food they supplied. My mom taught us to work hard and be grateful for what we had.

My mom didn't start dating again until we were grown. My youngest sister was a senior in high school when Mom had her first date. She had made a conscious decision to wait. I'm sure she was lonely. I can't imagine how much she missed my dad, her love and soulmate, but she didn't want to bring into our home the upheaval that can come from her dating or introducing a step-dad. She sacrificed for us. She quietly taught us that we were important, more important than any man she might meet. We were more important than her own happiness. I knew she loved me.

My mom's most valuable lessons were given in silence, by example. She also gave me a wicked penchant for Diet Coke and chocolate.

Cyndalynn Tilley

Cyndalynn is mom of three rambunctious kids. She is an RN and enjoys caring for those who are ill. She loves to read, mountain bike, knit and spend time with her kids. She actively volunteers and enjoys helping others.

Cyndalynn with her mother

college break flu

until i can draw a thin tube of sunlight back –
walk across college avenue in its academic garb
i am a child again in my mother's care

the cool heel of her hand on my forehead
her ordinary perfume mixes with cigarette breath
cough syrup vix vaporizer's misty steam
re-creates our one summer at a lake
white caps drain through clapping stones
and I sleep

frogmen light my 102.8 murky dreams with eyeball headlamps
a man jumps from an airplane
pulls the cord of his silky chute so he can reach
my bed in time to pin codified directions
of my secret mission to my pillow –

but my thrashes make me lose my place
somebody changes the code
her cool palm back on my forehead

Ron Bailey

ma

    in the 50's   at night
      on brighton ave
   second floor porch
         cars roll by
            radios on ---
   dewey hamlin's dog yaps at the end
of her rope across the street

      ma's cigarette smoke swirls ---
  ma holds me against her
        against her chest
    against her flowered night gown
i hear her heart beating
     up the stems
   out pink and yellow blossoms

        fingers on my cheek
   lips kiss the top of my short hair
     sun-browned summer head

      she gardens my drifting off to sleep
  i am a packet of seeds in her arms
      my feet take root in her lap

    daisies and pansies rub my ear . . .
      i fall to dreams with her melodies

Ron Bailey

My son Jared allowing me to hold his hand as I drive him home. Close contact is a struggle for him but he allows me to hold his hand for a few minutes. I taught him that at least.

Jerri Lynn Sparks

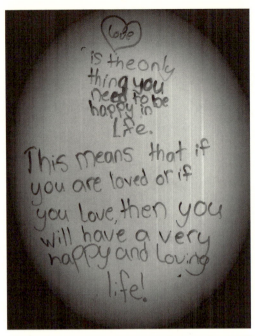

Katelynn Vukosic, Age 9

We all have special things we say to our children daily, whether it be as we tuck them into bed or before sending them off to school. Katelynn and I have had a regular saying for quite a few years. We have added to the popular "I love you to the moon and back" phrase. We say, "I love you to the moon and back, I love you to the sun and back, I'll meet you at the stars."

My amazing, smart, insightful, old soul, intuitive-beyond-her-years daughter said that there needs to be more than just the moon, sun and stars because she loves me more than those three things. It's times like those moments that I realize just how lucky, blessed and thankful I am.

As a side note, KL wrote the above note when she was sent to her room for fighting with her brother. Talk about thinking about why you are being punished and what you can do to make things better!

Kay Vukosic (Katelynn's Mom)

Mom Taught Me to Be Responsible

Always turn the light off

It was 6:00 when my mom called me to supper. "Dinner's ready!" she shouted so I could hear her in the basement. I ran upstairs and took my seat at one end of the table, my dad across from me, my brother to my right.

"Hello? Is anybody there?" my mom yelled into the basement. My dad looked at me accusingly. My brother snickered because this time it wasn't him.

I heard the flick of the light switch. Then she came to the table and gave me the look. That look every mom has that silently says, *Dear child, I love you. But how many times do I have to tell you? Turn the light off when you leave the room.*

This happened a lot. In the bathroom. The bedroom. The stairway. "Hello? Is anybody there?" It was my mom's refrain every time one of us left a light on in a room devoid of human beings.

Lights are powered by electricity. Electricity costs money. And money, as every kid learns at a young age, doesn't grow on trees.

One day recently, my three-year-old left the bathroom light on after using the potty. When I noticed the sliver of light underneath the door, I walked over, turned the handle, and shouted inside, "Hello? Is anybody there?" It was instinctive, an almost out-of-body experience, like when Patrick Swayze took over Whoopi Goldberg's psyche in the movie "Ghost."

It was then that I realized I am my mother's daughter. My mom was teaching us more than how to operate a light switch. She taught us more important lessons: Think before you act. Focus. Be respectful and responsible. Don't be wasteful.

My mom passed away in 2006, and it felt like all the lights went out. After a while, they slowly came back on and the darkness faded. Unfortunately, my mom didn't get to meet her two grandchildren, one who often does and one who someday will, forget to turn lights off. But I feel her smile in that I-told-you-so kind of way when I ask, "Hello? Is anybody there?" and no one answers.

Krista Gleason

Krista Gleason is a freelance writer and owner of Gleason Writes. She lives in Canandaigua, N.Y. with her husband, two children, and two pocket beagles who bark a lot.

Mom and Me
Krista Gleason

Live within your means and you will have the means to live

My mother was the second child of eight in a farm family. They lived out in the "middle of nowhere." There were two boys and six girls, so most of the girls handled the heavy work, too. My mother was one exception, because she was thin-boned and frail.

The farm house did not have running water and it was heated solely by a pot-bellied stove. They had a bit of land and a cow that provided milk for the family. Some of the land grew grain, hay and straw for the cow. A small patch of land grew family vegetables. The rest was cultivated for potatoes to sell.

Despite being poor, my mother was raised knowing education was key to success in life. After earning her high school diploma, my mother moved in with an aunt and uncle when she landed her first clerical job in a city some distance away.

At the age of 23, she married a security guard. Their first house was on the outskirts of the city and did not have running water, but it was within their income. An outhouse was nothing new to her anyway.

Because her husband was Roman Catholic, she agreed to become one, too. Ten months later my brother was born. Eleven months after that my sister was born. Nine months after that, my mother recognized she was pregnant again and the family was still using an outhouse. In the southern states, this might be okay, but in New York State, winters can be frigid. Taking toddlers to the outhouse could be quite a production and began to take up too much time, so my family moved into the city – into a house with running water!

My mother thought all her problems were solved. It was easier to do the laundry, bathing, and cleaning. My father could walk half a block and grab a bus to work. The move also meant my mother could go back to work and help with the mortgage.

After I, the third child, was born, my mother decided to use birth control. Of course that meant she was no longer welcome in the Catholic Church, but my Dad couldn't argue. He didn't go to church anyway.

As the months passed, my father started coming home later. He always grabbed a beer out of the refrigerator immediately. My mom assumed the lateness was caused by a change in the bus schedule. She was much too busy working all day and then taking care of two toddlers and an infant to greet him at the door each day. He arrived home later and later as time passed. He also contributed less and less money from his paychecks to pay the bills.

When she had had enough of this situation, my mom put the children to bed and sat in the living room with the radio off. As soon as she heard his footsteps on the front porch, she rushed to the front door. Whew! He reeked of beer already. Is that why he always grabbed a beer right away, to mask the ones he'd already drunk? When confronted, my father admitted that he and some bus companions were getting off a few blocks early and going to a bar. He promised to stop. He did for a short time, and then some more late arrivals home signaled a return to his problem.

My mother insisted they move out to a suburb. Since they only owned one car (normal in the 1950s), she would drop him off at work, then pick him up when she left her own work. Her boss was very nice, especially in those days. He let her adjust her hours to fit into her husband's schedule and was paid for the hours she worked. This worked well for a while.

Six years later, Mom had the "flu" again – a fourth child had been conceived. Her doctor had warned her that birth control pills could cause health problems if a woman stayed on them too long, so she had agreed to use abstinence during the hot times for six months, and then she could go back on them. Obviously, abstinence didn't work. Now the small house seemed even smaller. It could not handle another child. They had to move again. Bigger houses in the suburbs were much too expensive, so they moved back to the city, with Dad's promise to be good.

They found a house across the street from a hospital. My mom could work there and my Dad could use the car. This arrangement worked for a short time. Then he convinced my mother that gas was more expensive than bus fares.

You can guess what happened next.

When I was about 12, my Dad was finally kicked out of the house (after trying to kill my sister while drunk – but that is another story). After much coercion he agreed to pay $10 per week for child support. Even in the 1960s, this was a miniscule amount for four children.

Since Mom now had all the responsibilities 24/7, she handed me (again, about 12 at the time) Dad's $10, with instructions to get a whole week's worth of groceries, both food and toiletries. "Remember," she warned. "If your purchases don't last seven days, no one will be eating until the next $10 arrives." Although skeptical about my abilities, I felt honored that she had chosen me to do it, not my older brother or sister. Proudly, I managed to feed everyone for several months like this.

I don't remember when or why this stopped. Was it when I had two full time (80+ hours) babysitting jobs the summer of 1966? Anyway, this was not the first or last time my mother expected more of me than my siblings, when it came to money. At the age of 13, I paid for my own clothes and school supplies from money I earned babysitting. By the age of 16, I paid $10 a week rent to Mom from my part-time grocery store job.

At 17½, having graduated high school and working full time meant I bought groceries and contributed money toward bills. And then, I still paid for my own wedding (I proudly kept expenses at $50 even with 200 guests) and had saved the $1500 down payment for our first house.

There have been many times when my husband and I have had to scrimp and save. It has not always been easy. But at our

45th wedding anniversary, our house and two cars are debt-free. We probably have enough money saved to last the rest of our lives (knock on wood) and still leave some inheritance to the kids.

Thank you, Mom, for teaching me to spend wisely from a young age.

Karen Hockenberry

My mom and me

Karen Hockenberry

The List

The year was 1952. Marilyn had met her betrothed, Lloyd, at a party in Geneva on the Lake. His cousin Claire had introduced them. Marilyn and Lloyd were both the children of Hungarian Jewish immigrants. Her father was a housepainter; his was a roofer. She was 21 and pretty; he was 25 and athletic. Perfect. That's what they all thought. She wore a rented gown of white satin on that late November day, the day my parents got married.

Lloyd started work as an aluminum-siding salesman. Marilyn had had a year of college and loved it. But that was all her parents could afford. Now she was ready to start a family, as her older sister had. They bought a two-family house on Cedar Road near their parents' homes. It took five years, plus the insertion of a cervical ring, but finally a beautiful red-headed baby girl was born. Me.

Two years later, my sister entered the scene. And eleven months after that, my brother. For the next five years we lived in the lower half of that two-family house with only two bedrooms. My sister and I shared a room and our brother slept in the back porch. Of course this would not do. My mother had big plans. I watched each night as she pored over the blueprints for the new house she was having built for us on University Parkway. Even the street name sounded fancy.

When we finally moved into my mother's dream house, we couldn't believe how grand it seemed. Every room was carpeted in red plush! Our old living room furniture fit nicely into our new den which left our enormous new living room completely empty. We kids thought it was great - perfect for cartwheels and all sorts of fun.

More than a year went by and still no furniture. In retrospect, that was probably the first bad sign. Then one day they announced we would be moving again. That was the second bad sign. I was in fourth grade at Belvoir Elementary. We moved into a smaller house on a side street called White Road which, to my delight, shortened my walk to school. I had to share a room with my sister again, but I didn't mind. My mom set up our beds in an L-shape so our pillows were right near each other. We talked every night before falling asleep. And sometimes we spied on the old couple next door as they undressed for bed. Life was good, or so we thought.

My mom enrolled in classes at Western Reserve University, which meant she was never home when we came home for lunch. In the evenings she was always reading or typing at the kitchen table. Sometimes she played Helen Reddy's hit song, "I Am Woman," on our stereo console. That was probably the third bad sign.

My dad, for all his faults, was more available. On rainy days he'd pick us up from school and drive us home. I never wondered why he wasn't busy working.

The years went by that way until one spring day when my mom received her bachelor's degree in history education. I suppose that was the turning point. She took a couple of small jobs before landing the position of Workmen's Circle Director. From then on she must've saved every penny of every paycheck because before long she bought herself a black Oldsmobile Cutlass, her first car and her ticket to freedom, as she would later describe it. Then she divorced my father.

I should not have been so surprised that day when she stopped me on the stairs. I can't recall whether I was going up or down, but she caught me midway and told me the news. It shocked me to my core.

Though life as we knew it had come to an abrupt end, my life kept right on going. I found a boyfriend, went off to college, found a couple more boyfriends, graduated, was hired by the Eastman Kodak Company and moved to Rochester, found a few more boyfriends and had good times.

Ten years after my parents' divorce, my mother announced she was getting remarried. She'd met a man named Harry in a

Yiddish class. He was everything my father wasn't – educated, well-read, well-traveled, intellectual, supremely capable, hard-working and a man of culture. I could see that this list of qualities had become important to my mother, and that it had taken her a lifetime (my lifetime) to work them out.

I decided to make a list of my own. I started to look at the men I went out with in a more discerning way. I took my time. I wanted to get it right the first time.

My sister got married before me. And then my brother did. I was thirty-four years old when I finally said "I will" before a sanctuary filled with family and friends.

Despite our late start, Bill and I have created a beautiful family with three amazing kids. We've been married for over twenty-five years now. And it's been good. Really good. Occasionally Bill still teases me about that dreaded list of mine. But I know he's secretly proud to have been the one with enough check marks in the right column. After all, he won. And, thanks to my mother's hard-fought example, so had I.

Susan Baruch

Marilyn's graduation picture
Susan Baruch

ma was a counter

she tallied bills they could pay,
and poltergeists they hid in the desk --

she counted the days until christmas,
dollars until christmas,
clothes pins, coal deliveries, ice blocks up the back stairway,
hours before dad came back in the still dark of morning,
counted pennies,
my old shirts in attic bags a younger cousin might wear
someday,

she counted her brothers and sisters,
birthday candles, and funerals,
her son who died, among her blessings --
cups of coffee, grandma's sugar level,
pigeons on the drug store roof,
old gold cigarettes,
eight, nine, ten hailing a tv knockout

she counted her change for sunday offering,
stations of the cross,
the commandments,
people who sat in hunger in back pews,
the hail marys in her penance

at the end, she counted the same things again and again and
again,
never getting to ten,
losing track of the count

ma counted

Ron Bailey

Mothers know best (sometimes)

For years I simply thought my mother was mean. When I was almost 13, I spent every day at the beginning of January trying to convince my mother to let me have what is now called a "friends" birthday party. After two weeks of this, my mother relented, with the stipulation that the party be immediately after school and end before she came home from work. She further stipulated that I had to do all the preparation and clean up the house afterwards. Yay!

That year, I learned how much work goes into a party, including figuring out the guest list, writing invitations, menu planning, and food prep. I did all that work with pleasure. I had everything ready for the party the night before it was to happen.

Then the evening news warned that a blizzard was expected that night and schools were already cancelled for the next day. Shucks! "Oh well," I remember thinking, "I can shovel a path to all my friends' houses so they can get to my party." I went to bed early so I could get the shoveling done early.

When I woke up the next morning, everything was white outside and snow was still falling. I dressed quickly and ran outside with the shovel. I managed to clear the front porch, steps, and the path leading to the main sidewalk, in about half an hour. Geesh! This was heavy snow! Since each friend lived a few blocks away – in opposite directions – my plans slowly melted, like I wished the snow would. Alas, it didn't. It just kept falling from the sky.

I stood at the end of the short path and noticed that the beginning of the path was already filled with snow. "Maybe my friends won't mind trudging through the snow," I thought, as I went inside to warm up a little.

As I ate breakfast, my friends began to call to say they couldn't get through the snow. I understood, but was still devastated. After all, this was the first and probably only time my mother would allow a "friends party." All the others had just immediate family members.

I moped around the house the rest of the day. Snow was still falling when my mother arrived home at suppertime. (We lived across the street from the hospital where she worked). She told us that most people had not been able to get into work, so the hospital was working with a skeleton crew. The people who worked with the patients were sleeping at the hospital and working whenever they were awake.

The clerks who made it in to work could go home, but everyone would still need to be paid, as would the bills. Since no end was in sight to this freak blizzard, the hospital needed every able body and mind to help. Therefore, my sister could help in the business office and I could help in my Mom's payroll office.

Wow!!! This blizzard would be fun after all!

Schools were closed the whole week. During that time, I filed time cards and sorted hundreds of checks for the bank reconciliation. Loved it! I also loved the free lunch given to any volunteer who worked eight hours. I could choose as much as I wanted and whatever I wanted. That was a very memorable week. Besides being able to act like an adult, I also had dessert with every lunch, which didn't happen at home. Heavenly!

This was my first experience where a "tragedy" turned into an opportunity, and my whole attitude changed about the setbacks in life. I began to appreciate my mother a little more, too. I was a teenager, so I can't say I began to behave properly at all times, but at least my teen behavior was tempered with more respect toward my mother.

Thank you, Mom. You did know best in 1966!

Karen Hockenberry

Oops!

My Momma taught me not to bring stuffed animals to the table

One day when I was five, I was sitting at the table with my favorite stuffy, Giraffe, tucked behind my back. We were having peas and chicken. I didn't like peas, so I had to keep taking gulps of milk. Then when I noticed my milk cup was empty, I reached over my plate to push the nearly-empty cup to Mom so she could fill it up for me. But ... oops! It tipped. It spilled.

I jumped out of the way, but when I did that there was no one to block Giraffe from getting wet. When I realized what had happened, I quickly grabbed Giraffe and raced her to the washing machine. Thankfully, we could run a load.

At bedtime, Mom came up and told me that Giraffe was still in the dryer and she would bring it to me when it was done. "Okay," I said. But it really wasn't. I would never ever bring any stuffed animals to the table again.

Kayla Wells, age 10

Passing on the love of reading
Aaron Wells

All opinions matter ~ Let your voice be heard

My momma taught me to let my opinion shine through the fog. I am proud to be an American who lives in a country where voices and opinions matter. It doesn't matter if we all agree. In fact, it is highly unlikely we will all agree. On just about anything. And that is glorious.

When I was young, my mom would often say, "We're not arguing. We're discussing." That discussion of opinions may have been quite heated now and then, and other folks might have called it yelling at each other sometimes, but we were always discussing, not arguing. We never hit, pulled hair, shoved, that sort of physicality of arguments. We still respected each other's ability to think for ourselves. We just didn't agree on the particulars. I didn't understand why I needed to make my bed so dog hair wouldn't suffocate me at night, or take shorter showers so I didn't use up all the hot water in the tank before everyone had taken their showers. I disagreed that I needed to come back to the house when Mom called us in for dinner and I was half a mile away in the woods and Mom was going a bit crazy with worry. Ya' know. The mundane human stuff.

Everyone is entitled to her own opinion in this country. Unfortunately, some people choose to shout their uncompromising opinions to the masses, while others choose a more mild-tempered route and quietly discuss important matters, following the rules of peaceful engagement, as at a dinner table or a meeting room table. Respect and responsibility toward ourselves and each other is an essential part of humanity. It allows us to tackle the less mundane human elements. When a very close aunt and uncle were having marital issues and ultimately divorced when my cousins were little, Mom modeled responsibility in keeping her opinions on their personal affairs to herself and offering more objective support to the other household instead of fueling their conflict.

Mom by no means kept her opinions to herself, though. When there was an issue, especially when it came to her cubs and their treatment at school or in the community, for instance, Momma Bear came out in force. However, that Momma Bear was objective, restrained, respectful. She knew whom she needed to speak to in order to resolve the issue of a 4th grader's two hour daily homework time. She used her knowledge and respectful, powerful persuasion to affect change.

Within our extended family, everyone knows Aunt Karen is the "crazy" one who will wear what she wants to wear, do what she wants to do, say what she means, and does what she says she's going to do. The light-hearted moniker does not mean she's actually considered mentally unstable. She's unique. We respect her for always doing what's best for her family, the community, the school, whatever situation she finds herself in. She has developed a strong sense of discussion and persuasion.

Once when I lied (well, failed to tell her) about a particular social tidbit the summer after high school graduation, instead of flipping out when she found out from another mom, she took a few minutes to quietly reflect, made notes on what to speak with me about, and then proceeded to come to me about the offense. She still didn't blow up. She spoke with calm seriousness that was actually much more powerful than a blow up would have been. It scared the bejeebers out of me, and I never committed that offense ever again. Mom knew the power of words, and knew when she needed to temper her words with reflection.

My husband and I have openly discussed our opinions on politics, religion, society at large, even the miniscule gossipy sort of small town news, everything, at the dinner table and beyond. I hope we are benefitting, not scarring, our children in the process. I don't really remember Mom discussing the news of the day or heavy stuff at the dinner table, but then again, I remember my dad worked long hours for much of my childhood, so without another adult to converse with most of the time, pressing childhood topics reigned. However, it was our nightly tradition to always say something good that happened each day, and I feel we did discuss the bad stuff that happened too, but humans tend to repress negative memories, so I can't really remember much negative discussion around the table.

The strangulation of my favorite middle school teacher only weeks after I took her class made us pause and rationally reflect on the dark side of the world, but even in that instance, I was allowed to think, to breathe, to reflect internally or aloud, and be heard wherever I was. I was able to heal as I processed the information, and of course Mom encouraged me to join my friends and participate in the service held in town the following week. But that was really the extent of my negative view from small town America.

My life was not filled with the daily trauma, the drama that unfolds in many households and communities across the country. We had material comforts, we had friends and family around us, we had a good education system, extracurriculars to keep us busy, chores to develop our responsibility. We were comfortable. I had quite an insular childhood, but when something did hit home, we discussed it openly. My parents allowed us to think and process things as we were, and were ready whenever we wanted or needed a sounding board. By the time my brother and I were in high school and Global Studies class forced us to reflect weekly on world events, we were becoming conditioned to listen to and respect other people's points of view, especially if we wanted ours to be heard and respected.

We need to come together as a community of human beings who share this precious Earth and want to see it survive and thrive for the next generations. We need to stop arguing for the sake of arguing, as my mom also often said. We need to come together to discuss opinions, problems and potential solutions. I don't care what political party you favor, what religious or cultural system you subscribe to. I don't care if you agree with me or not. That's not the point. That's actually fabulous. When diverse people come together for a common good, only good comes from it. As long as we respect and love. When diverse people come together with uncompromising views of politics or of economy or of ANY part of this gift called life, that's when we have conflict we may not survive.

My mom taught me to appreciate opinions even if they differ from my own. Wouldn't life be so boring if we all were the same?! I feel so blessed by all the thoughts and opinions I hear and read around me every day. We live in a beautiful country, rich with diverse populations, where we can feel free to express our opinions on the mundane or the enormous topics. This is largely what drives me forward in my academic pursuits.

I have read, edited, analyzed, and taught many powerful pieces from many walks of life across the globe. I specifically focused on non-traditional literature in grad school. I love reading stories by people who have such different experiences than I. Everyone has a unique story to tell. We can't squash anyone's story, anyone's truth. If we do, then they may do the same to ours, and where would we be then? Story-less? Truth-less? Since they are our life stories, would that make us Life-less? Self-less (and not the good *selfless*)? Would anything we have done even matter, if we are suddenly gone?

I taught for a year in a middle school full of students with a very different worldview than I had, and I appreciated the differences between our beliefs. And yet, we are so similar. People are people, no matter what color their skin, accent in their speech, opinions on politics or religion, and we must speak our own stories, our own opinions. We must listen to others' stories, their opinions. We cannot get bogged down in harassing bigotry. We must appreciate what each other brings to the table, discuss the greatness of humanity, and we must move our own futures forward.

We need to work together to make the world a better place! Such a cliché, but a cliché of the utmost importance. We each can make the world a better place by being our best selves each and every day. We need to listen to those who are different than we are. We need to speak up for ourselves and what we feel is just and kind, responsible for all involved or affected and compassionate toward all elements of the situation. All opinions matter. All people matter, and all people must work together to discuss problems, to make the world a better place despite and because of our differences.

We can! My mom taught me so.

Sueann Wells

Mom taught me to think carefully when two paths diverge
Sueann Wells

Work hard

My mother came from a farm family with eight children. They all rose early, did their chores, and then walked a few miles to school. When they returned, they all had chores to accomplish before they could eat supper. Being children, they frequently made a game of each chore, such as who could bring in the most firewood, or who could fill the water bucket fullest and bring it in without spilling anything. My mother was the frailest child. Although she tried hard, she just couldn't beat her more robust siblings. Homework after supper was a welcome relief from the physical work. This was when my mom shined. She always finished first and then helped the younger siblings with theirs.

With this background, when my mother married at the age of 23, she was no stranger to hard work. To stay within their income, my parents bought a house in a suburb with no running water. Two years later she had already birthed two children. She rinsed the diapers in a pail of water, then dumped it down the hole of the outhouse. She then washed diapers and baby clothes with a scrub board in a pail of water heated on the stove.

When expecting a third child (the others were 1½ and 2½ when the third was born), the family moved into the city and then had running water. This freed up some time, so my mother worked full time to help with the new mortgage. Full-time work for a woman in the 1950s and 1960s did not pay well, but the money did help make a dent in the budget for a short time and became the majority of bill-paying funds later, when her husband began to spend most of his paycheck on alcohol.

Besides the smaller pay for a lot of work, she also had to deal with a society that frowned upon women working full-time when they should be home with their children. The "great war" was over, after all. I can remember my mother's friends talking about how some problem may not have happened if my mother had been home. When I told my mother what I had heard, she just shrugged and said, "Don't worry about what other people say. Other people simply don't understand our life." She didn't drop any of those friends, but she didn't change what she was doing, either.

To me, my mother had grit and was willing to do whatever it took to make sure her four children had warm shelter, adequate clothing, and food in their bellies. I can remember my mother worked six days a week to accomplish this. By that time, the oldest three kids were in our early teens, so we had the responsibility of keeping the house in order and watching our youngest sibling, who was in primary school.

My older brother was in charge of the yard, mowing and snow removal. My sister and I were in charge of laundry, dishes, vacuuming, ironing, and general cleaning. Perhaps it is a memory problem, but I cannot remember my older sister actually doing housework. Many days she simply came home from school too late to complete them. I remember performing all the above tasks myself.

Through it all we never suffered from unfulfilled REAL need. And as for the housework, whenever I complained, Mom simply stated, "Life doesn't owe you anything. You must work hard unless you physically can't anymore." Even without prodding, she'd say, "Work comes before play in life."

Thank you, Mom. Now that I'm in my 60s, all the years I've worked hard are beginning to pay off. Now I can slow down a little, at least on the housework.

Karen Hockenberry

Mom Taught Me to Be the Best I Can Be

Finding a good melon

The sun was shining brightly in 1970s western North Carolina, and a huge field of watermelons enticed us from across our tiny dirt road. Passing cars threw up dust clouds every few minutes so we couldn't see the other side of the road, making it seem as though we lived in a haze of uncertainty. I think maybe we were living more precariously than I realized as a child.

My mother sat on the front steps with my little sister and me, her long legs bent up underneath her as she rested her auburn-covered head in her hands. I remember she had these long, strong, artistic fingers, just like her father, my beloved Paw Paw, and I always thought those were hands that could do anything. I think it's redeeming and incredibly beautiful how a child's mind imbues people, places and experiences with such magical attributes.

We all peered out at the day, my mother, my sister, and me, just trying to figure out what we were going to do. My mom seemed so grownup to me then but in reality she was only twenty-two years old with two kids, a husband, a full-time job, and a house to manage. When I was twenty-two I had just moved to California and had hardly a care in the world. My fingers were long and strong like hers, but I didn't yet have any idea what my hands were going to do in life. It would be years before I realized the lovely symbolism that my hands write my heart, and those hands were inherited from her and my heart was most certainly shaped by her…

My sister and I, being so little on that hot summer day, really were more concerned with which Big Wheels car we were going to ride along the driveway, but my mother seemed to have something more troubling on her mind. This would be a theme I'd encounter many times in my childhood as my mother's mind long remained an enigma to me. She'd get this far away look in her eyes and pull out her pack of cigarettes, Marlboro's in a red pack if I remember correctly. As a young child this didn't bother me because it was just what she did and I knew nothing else.

Everyone smoked down South when I was a kid, even teachers and pastors.

As years passed, I came to hate those "cancer sticks," as I call them, and I would hide them from her, causing her to scream at me and threaten me with all sorts of punishment until I caved and reluctantly handed certain death back to her aging hands. It breaks my heart to see her once beautiful hands now creased with the detritus of nicotine and smoke. I can only imagine the horrors done to her lungs. She made us all promise never to try them and none of her three children smoke. (Sometimes parents teach us what not to do by example).

"Do you girls want to go pick out a watermelon?" my mom suddenly asked, breaking the hot and stagnant silence. "Yes!" we both gleefully cried out as we took off running barefoot toward the field of watermelons without waiting for her.

I remember the three of us walking along the rows, carefully rolling each watermelon over to see if it was ripe, trying hard not to rip it off the vine. I had no idea what I was doing but I was certain my mother knew what she was doing. Don't all little children think that of their parents?

Finally we settled on what we all deemed to be a good melon and carefully picked it off the vine. The walk back across the road from that scorching field with this big old watermelon in our arms seemed to take an hour. By the time we got back to the front steps of our house, we were all drenched in sweat.

Mom went inside and got a big kitchen knife, and immediately began slicing into the watermelon right there on the front steps. My sister and I stood back in eager anticipation. We could see the juice running out where the knife was piercing the melon and my mouth began to water. It was so hot outside and I wanted that juicy watermelon so badly. There is nothing like sweet watermelon on a hot Southern day.

Finally the melon was split in half, and my mother sank to the ground and began crying. I was so confused.

"What's wrong, mommy?" I asked hesitantly.

"It's not ripe," she said sadly and threw up her hands in

defeat.

And with that my mom went back inside, letting the screen door slam behind her. I could hear her crying softly in the kitchen. My sister and I just looked at each other in bewilderment. I went over and picked up the melon and tried to take a bite of it but it tasted awful. Even the ants were keeping their distance from it.

There was no saving that melon.

A few minutes later my mom came outside dressed to go out.

"Come on," she said confidently with the look of determination of someone who had had enough. She took us by the hands and put us in the car, one of those cool 1970s jalopies my grandpa had loaned us from his used car business. Mom had done her hair and makeup and had on those big glasses that made her look like a movie star. She popped us in the backseat (no car seats back then), turned up the radio, rolled down the windows (no automatic windows back then either) and took off driving. We made our own joyful cloud of dust that day.

"Where are we going?" my little sister and I asked, the wind blowing in our preschool hair, Credence Clearwater Revival filling our ears, both of us still mesmerized by what had just happened.

"We are going to get a *good* melon!" she said happily.

And that we did.

A short time later we moved into the house that would become my childhood home. Somehow that good melon hunt became the turning point in my mother's mind. Things fell in place after that one tiny battle, that one refusal to accept defeat. Whenever I hear "Proud Mary keep on burnin," I am immediately taken back to that day when the wind was like freedom and salvation to my mother and our journey was much more than the hunt for a good melon.

I think about this scene a couple times a year now that I'm a grownup raising my own kids by myself. My mother could have just accepted defeat that day, could have let that bad melon become a symbol of failure. She could have let the unknown malaise life sometimes threw at her take her down. She could have easily locked herself in her room and cried the rest of the day. But she didn't. And over and over many times I've seen my mom pull herself up from the metaphorical floor, and sometimes the literal one, and rise back up victorious. She takes uncertainty and smacks it in the face with those long fingers of hers.

Obviously, something else was on her mind that day on the front steps because it was never just about the bad melon. I never found out for sure what it was – I was too young to understand – but I think I now know since we moved from that house a few months later.

What my mother taught me is this: you protect your children from the bad things in life as much as you can. Your children are not your therapists and they are not your best friends, despite what so many people say. Our role as mothers, as parents, is to protect our children and prepare them for the world outside, to confidently handle bad days with a determined plan, with really good hair and uplifting music, so that we can confidently and happily bounce back from the bad melons and go out and find the good ones.

Jerri Lynn Sparks

Like mother, like daughter

My mother,
a blue star of second magnitude,
once taught me
how to tumble through the universe.
We were dwelling
then in the vast sway of time
just east
of Alula Borealis, so our shine too leapt
like a gazelle
in his northern sky. It was winter, time
of the Leonids.
That year's shower, a lighter one paled pearly by
a bright moon,
was observed from Earth in a temperate zone
by the man
her daughter had a long-flickering eye on.
My mother,
all blithe white rays in that night's sky,
instructed me
in the ways of dust motes of desire,
how like them
to shoot and burn the vast distances of love
ignited, flying
light years to land that December like a breath
on the back
of his neck. How I burned to touch him.
My mother,
wise in the odd manners of constellations,
and the human
minds that named them, reminded me he would
remember me
and the brief hot meteoric kiss I bestowed upon him.
My mother too
had once fallen for an astronomer, Galileo it was

I believe
they called him – another one with a yearning for
women like us.

Karla Linn Merrifield

A nine-time Pushcart-Prize nominee and National Park Artist-in-Residence, Karla Linn Merrifield has had over 500 poems appear in dozens of journals and anthologies. She has 12 books to her credit, the newest of which is Bunchberries, More Poems of Canada, *a sequel to* Godwit: Poems of Canada *(FootHills), which received the Eiseman Award for Poetry. She is assistant editor and poetry book reviewer for* The Centrifugal Eye, *a member of the board of directors of Just Poets (Rochester, NY), and a member of the New Mexico State Poetry Society and the Florida State Poetry Society. She is still looking for a home for* The Comfort of Commas, *a quirky chapbook that pays tribute to punctuation. Visit her woefully outdated blog, Vagabond Poet, at* <http://karlalinn.blogspot.com>.

Change a bad system from within

My mother always told us that violence or yelling doesn't really solve anything. To change a bad system, we should work within it, quietly and persistently. Then she showed us how to do it...

She took us to a very conservative church, in which rock music, drive-in movies, and facial make-up were all considered the devil's tools. Yet she also took us four children to the drive-in theater to see Elvis movies. We never talked about them at church, but we never hid our attendance either.

Though common conservative thought was that drive-ins encouraged "loose" behavior, most of the cars contained whole families, not romantic couples. In fact, there were even mini-playgrounds directly under the screens to keep children occupied and tire them out a little. That way, parents could enjoy the movies when the sky darkened. In the 1950s, we paid by the number of people over the age of 12 in the car, so when Mom took all of us, she only had to pay a nominal fee for herself, and it was an inexpensive family outing.

My mother also applied make-up whenever she was going out of the house, including when we went to church. She said we didn't have to agree with everything in a church in order to belong to it. The church just has to fill our need for God in our lives. After a couple years' attendance at this church, my mother became a deaconess. She really did change the system – without yelling or violence.

I remembered that lesson many years later. As a Sunday school teacher for two-four year-olds, I would sit in the sanctuary until the midpoint, and when the children left their seats to go to their classes I would walk out with anyone who came to my class, usually four year-olds. I would then pick up the two and three year-olds from the nursery and we would all go next door to our classroom.

One day, at the beginning of a service, I heard some older folks whispering behind me about a teenager who had just walked into the sanctuary wearing jeans. To me, having a teenager come to church at all was a blessing, yet these older folks were quite upset about their attire.

I was too shy to correct them verbally. Instead, the next Sunday I wore jeans to church myself. That first time, the stares and scowls abounded. Whew! If looks could kill…

Within a month or two, the scowls were gone. Either they didn't care anymore or they had resigned themselves to having a quirky Sunday school teacher. Either way, I never again heard nasty whispering about someone's clothing.

Thanks, Mom. It worked!

Karen Hockenberry

Take time to rest

"Mawhmm," my brother Ben whines, even though he is almost eight.

"We're not three anymore, Mom," I add, with more attitude in my voice than I truly intend. Hey, a little 'tude is better than whining, right? Why does Mom always have us lay down to nap – 'rest' as she calls it? It's summer time, our daycare friends are here, and we all reenergized ourselves with that tasty lunch of PB&J and BBQ chips. Now we're all ready to get back outside to climb trees and play in the fort we made simply fantastic this morning. It beckons for us to return. And yet she makes us all split up to different rooms and rest for an hour. Every. Single. Day. Bah!

Ben sticks out his jaw and I put my hands on my hips. All to no avail.

"I don't want to hear it," Mom says firmly, some would even say loudly. "We play hard all day. We rest after lunch." And that is that. She flings a pillow at my feet. I kick at it. We dance this dance every day. Why would today be any different? I try anyway.

"But WHY, Mawhm?" The whine enters my seven-year-old voice. I know my BFF in the next room can hear me. The daycare buddies don't even bother fighting this oppressor anymore. Mom actually put a bar of soap in Mike's mouth last week because he cursed for a third time despite warnings. They all know Mom means business. Alas, Ben and I are alone. We'll fight the good fight. Right?

"We want to go back outside! Why can't we?" I say more maturely, my head up, shoulders back, standing strong, assertive but not aggressive, my swelling ego ready to persuade her with reason and rational thought.

Then I hear the No nonsense tone and avert my eyes from the No nonsense glare only Mom can give. "Because I said so." She turns on her heels and marches out to make sure the others have their pillows or blankets.

I give up. I lay down on the super-thin, super-small, maybe three foot diameter crimson area rug in the playroom, my dungeon cell for the hour. It is no use arguing further. The end of July now, we have been trying to convince Mom to abolish rest time nearly every day for a month. There was that one time Ben fell asleep on the ride home from bowling in town, and that other rainy day Mary Ellen and I both drifted off during an afternoon movie. But other than that, we are always raring to go and are squelched by Dictator Mom who must just want us to go back to school.

I look around the play room. Why don't I get to stay in my own room, for heaven's sake? Can't the baby – toddler, whatever he is – Can't he set up in here? He's going to mess with all my stuff. Ben at least gets to rest in his own room. Just because I'm younger and *can* lie on the floor doesn't mean I *should*. It's not fair.

'Life's not fair,' Mom would say. Bah! She's in my head. I reach a silent hand out toward the set of blocks piled against the wall. My fingers itch to play, even with these baby toys, but I hear Mom's waterbed sloshing about. She's getting comfortable. She will simply be a bear if I bother her now. I can't make a single sound. I hold my breath and start counting. I let it out after only a few seconds. This won't be fun for long.

I close my eyes. Silent fun, silent fun. Not like the times when I put small papers on the hallway floor where the boards creak, thinking I was being sneaky. How sneaky was it really when the papers said outright, "Don't step ~ It creaks," and every time someone walked by, the draft blew around all the papers, and I had to do it all again? Silent fun this time, silent fun, silent …

My muscles relax and I fall asleep even on this hard floor in this dreadfully boring rest time in my dungeon cell.

"Little Sue" (as the caption on the photo's back says) taking a rest way back when, evidently with my sneakers still on

Karen Hockenberry

    Momma always had us rest, especially on long, hot summer days, and especially whenever my Dad worked long hours as an insurance salesman or as an Army recruiter. Mom was the primary caregiver for a solid 12-14 hour 'workday' six days those weeks. And in addition to my brother and me, Mom also had between two and six other children at our house for daycare any given weekday.

    Now that I am mother to three lovely children, and have also spent the past nine years providing daycare to other families, I understand her need for rest. I never really allowed myself rest as the girls grew up. I never was one to follow the directions in the new momma books that say to rest when the baby rests. Let's face it; that works for the first child, but once that second child comes into the household, this Momma anyway wanted to spend the baby-downtime bonding with the older child. And once the third child comes? Yeah, Momma's not resting ever during the day. I can rest when they're older, I'd tell myself.

Some of my friends successfully had Rest time for their non-napping children. For them, it worked. They'd have a solid hour or two to breathe, to read grown-up novels (I certainly did not read much besides the kids' books I read all day every day for a few years there), to simply veg and unwind, to reenergize themselves. I was quite envious, to be honest. I tried to make it work in my household, but ended up having toddler/momma battles that wore me out even more, so I gave up the effort, knowing there would come a time when all were sleeping through the night and I could find time for me again.

When my youngest was born, I did finally institute Rest time during the day, right after lunch when she and daycare nappers went upstairs, but our Rest time meant me reading books to or with the older kids, doing puzzles, writing, drawing, all quiet activities, but still awake "On" Momma time.

My weary mom evidently took a photo of me in my usual rest time place in the playroom when I was almost five, and though I can't verify it because I was little and my testy little self would never admit it even if I did remember it, I am told I often fell asleep during rest time. We all did. Evidently. So Momma says.

Now, at 35, I appreciate that. Countless times, I have had to make a choice for my child or my children, skipping some social opportunity, or cutting short evening activities, simply because I see them turning to pumpkins and I know rest is best at that moment. We need our rest to be our best selves. We play hard all day. We rest after lunch ... Or, whenever we need to or can.

My momma taught me to take time to rest, that the hustle and bustle of daily life wears at you if you don't take a break, even if that break is a break from fun stuff like climbing trees and running around with friends. Everyone needs a break to function at her best.

Now that none of my children takes naps (it's been a good three years, I'd say), and now that even my youngest joins in the pretend play of her sisters and I don't have to mediate quite as often, I have stepped back a bit. I appreciate the time to write and read and enjoy life. I still have a long to-do list. But I know to take time to rest, time to enjoy my own hobbies just for the sake of my hobbies and my own mental health.

I am a worrier. I got that from my mom as well, I guess. I stress about things a lot of people seem not to stress about. I wish I could be more easy-going, a fly-by-the-seat-of-my-pants kind of mom, but I suppose I'm not going to learn that from my mom. I am just like my mom in many ways. I am human, a work in progress, and I will continue to strive to be more like her in her ability to take a rest when she needs to. Stop everything. Life will not end if I don't finish a project. All will be okay, and in fact, Life will be more enjoyable because I will be more rested and ready to tackle whatever comes my way.

Sueann Wells

*Freelance editor and writer, Sueann Wells, mother of three, who has taught at the Elementary through College levels, is looking to make her way back into the post-secondary world. She has written and published regularly even in her recent 'hiatus' home with her young children. Wells has been published in journals, newspapers, magazines, and encyclopedias, presented at literary conferences, and has had two poetry collections published through FootHills Publishing (*Midnight Summons *(2006),* Awake Before Dawn *(2009)). She has dabbled in the creative side of self-publishing her own poetry collection (*Seasons of Life: A year of linked cinquains *(2013)) and children's books (*Stone Soup: Suburban Style, *and her mom's* Dinosaur Parade*), and working with contributors and publishers to create the* Mother Muse *(2009) and* Motherly Musings *(2011, Unlimited) collections. Wells loves sharing powerful creative writing with the world, and embraces every chance to work with great writers to do so. Email her at* RochesterNYEditor@yahoo.com.

Taking a vacation from me

From the age of about six through my early teen years, I remember going to church at the very least on Sunday mornings and Thursdays after school every week. In the summer there were also two weeks of Vacation Bible School. On the few occasions we traveled, we always had to find a church nearby and spend time at their services. If we complained, my mother would scold, "We are lucky that God doesn't take a vacation from us. He is here for us all day, every day. We can certainly find a couple of hours to spend at His house." Similar logic took us to church services even when we felt ill. To my young mind, I thought we had to be on our death bed to stay home from Sunday morning services.

I can remember one morning when a general malaise overshadowed all my actions. There was no point in telling my mother how I felt, so I dressed and left for church with my family. Breakfast had been our own responsibility for years, so my mother didn't notice my lack of eating.

Sunday School went without any major problems. I just felt "spacey" and couldn't pay attention. I had always been painfully shy so my teacher didn't notice the extra quietness. After Sunday School, regular services began, with my siblings and I sitting in the sanctuary near my mother. I wore a slight smile – a little smug I had made it that far. Only an hour to go….

Then, in the middle of a hymn, the malaise hit me full-force. The room spun in circles; my knees felt spongy. I grabbed the back of the pew in front of us and sat down quickly, closing my eyes in the process.

My mother jabbed me on the shoulder. I opened my eyes and saw her scowl. In a whisper, I told her I didn't feel well. She whispered back, "Go to the car and lay down, then, but you will be in your bed the rest of the day."

In her motherly mind, she probably thought that was a punishment for a wayward pre-teen. I don't blame her. My older brother and sister had used many, many excuses to try to stay home. That day, I did not. To this day, I don't know if I was running a fever that Sunday. Probably. I did sleep most of that day and through the night.

Then I entered my teen years…. As soon as I entered high school, homework compounded exponentially, mainly because I was in Honors classes. The additional homework was an acceptable excuse to skip Thursday afternoon youth group and evening prayer meetings. Sunday mornings continued to be mandatory.

Once I left my mother's home as an adult, I continued the Sunday morning routine for a short time. Then I changed jobs, since a factory worker made more money than a bank teller, and my husband and I had bills to pay. The factory work included many Saturdays and some Sundays. When I didn't work on Sunday, I wanted to sleep a little later. I watched a church service on the television, which enabled me to sleep until 10AM.

When my kids were born, I took them to a church nearby for a while. Then my infant daughter came home from the nursery with a big goose-egg and there was an inadequate explanation from the nursery volunteer as to how it happened. Thus, I returned to watching church on TV.

As my children grew enough to talk to me, I again made Sunday morning church a priority in life. Happy with the spiritual instruction given to my kids, I even taught Sunday school. This continued for many years. I don't think I ever made church mandatory, but since we lived out in the country, my children liked the interaction with the other children who came to church.

Then my children hit their teens. The leader of the young teen group did some things that went against my principles, so I returned to church on TV.

With some brief interludes of actually going to church, I basically liked getting more free time to do other things. I could watch the church service in my pajamas, or dress and prepare for some event and just take an hour break to watch.

At the beginning of my sixth decade of life, a slight OCD that had plagued me all my life grew and grew almost to the point of phobia. I tried to just read the Bible and pray more, but it wasn't enough. I was down 40+ pounds and still losing weight. Maybe this was something physical. My doctor ordered a lot of tests, but found nothing wrong. Then a psychologist tried to correct the situation. Still the OCD grew.

Although eating more than my husband, my weight went down to 116 pounds (I weighed more than that when I was 13 years old). My ribs could be counted easily from a distance. Nighttime sleep was limited to a maximum of four hours. I was desperate. This monster could not continue to grow much longer. My body and mind simply couldn't take much more of this. I stopped at a local church one weekday, expecting … oh I don't know what I expected…

A women's group was meeting in a large room as I walked to the church office. After hearing that I needed to speak to the minister about a problem, the secretary went into the large room and an older woman walked out to speak with me. She spoke in a Scottish brogue and seemed very nice.

She and I set up a time to meet privately. Because of my own schedule, the meeting would take place when the church was closed and the minister was usually preparing the next Sunday's service and sermon. I was not a church member, nor even a participant, yet she was willing to give up some of her private time for me.

The meeting with her lifted my spirits immensely. She agreed with some things I had said and done. I wasn't going crazy! She also stated that there was nothing wrong with taking prescriptions to help me with my budding phobias, as I worked on my coping skills. As she said, "For physical problems, you sometimes need to take a pill. What is different about a mental problem?" It didn't mean that God had abandoned me. She never emphasized that I should come to her church, though she did mention it in passing as I left that private meeting. I walked to my car with a bounce in my step. Perhaps I would check out the Sunday morning service…

A man in Scottish plaid greeted me with a smile at the church entrance. Two more people greeted me warmly at the top of the inside staircase. Another person greeted me at the entrance to the sanctuary. I sat near the back to observe as much as possible. This also meant that many people welcomed me as they walked up to their usual seats.

While waiting for the service to begin, I read the four-page bulletin. Jeesh, this was an active church! In addition to the normal Bible study and prayer meetings, there were social times like dinners, luncheons, festivals, a cake walk, and even a Euchre tournament. Also on the weekly calendar were visitations to the jail, homeless shelters, and nursing homes. Or parishioners could help glean vegetables from nearby farms to give to the local food cupboard, or help cook/deliver Sunday dinners for/to the shut-ins. I said a quick prayer thanking God for leading me to this particular church.

The rest is now history. Most Sunday mornings now find me at church. Occasionally, I go to the meditative prayer meetings. The "cake walk" and Euchre tournaments are included in my social calendar, as are some of the women's group meetings. My weight is at a more healthy level. A minimum dosage of medication is still part of my daily routine, but it is so little the doctor can't believe it helps at all. I'm not totally worry-free, but isn't that a natural part of being an adult? However, when today is compared to those troubling months, my worry level is much lower.

Thanks, Mom, for teaching me that physically attending a church is important for our health. And thank you, God, for not taking a vacation from me.

Sue Vogt

Karen Hockenberry

Me and my mom Sue celebrating life
Heidi Banser

Mother Eva

My mother, Eva, taught me so many things in my journey as a girl, a wife and a mother. Three lessons stand out:

 *Give back to the community
 *Make good choices
 *Take care of family

I was the firstborn, eldest of seven children. While it is a prestigious birth order, it is also one with great responsibility. I often heard comments like, "You are the oldest. You set the example for your two brothers and four sisters. You will go to college and lead the way for them to follow." No pressure, right?

My mom was a wonderful role model and teacher. She had a loving and kind spirit. My mother would visit the sick and shut-in neighbors in our community. She would bring a casserole, a plant or one of her handcrafted dolls to spread cheer and well wishes. This left its mark on me and generations after me. Like my mom, we often volunteer, serve on committees and Boards of Directors, and donate to charities. Starting at an early age, our children served in soup kitchens, walked in charity marathons, and collected coats and mittens for the homeless. Eva's lesson of community service continue to echo throughout her family.

"Make good choices!" These words were always heard from my mother whenever any of us left the house to go to school, church, work, or on dates. It was as though our mom had a cloak of wisdom she placed on our shoulders and whispered in our ears. As we grew older, we were able to keep those words in mind as the choices became more difficult. Even today, my children remind each other and my grandchildren, Kennedy and Emerson, to make good choices.

From my mother, I learned at an early age what it means to take care of family. As young children we enjoyed spending time with each other and "having each other's back." I was often called the "other mother." My siblings knew they could count on me to take care of them. My example was my mother and the ways she always found time to spend with each of us. She made us feel important as she listened to our stories and adventures. She knew our likes and dislikes, our favorite things to do and our love language. I didn't know how she kept everything straight with her seven children.

Now, as a mother myself, I understand. It is because of the love a mother has for her children. They are each special in their own way. As my mother modeled in her family, I enjoy knowing what my five children like, their favorite things, and how they feel loved. It comes from spending time and listening to each child.

My mother taught me a family works together and supports each other. As a result, we enjoy being together and keeping in touch. We look forward to birthday parties, reunions, picnics, and weddings. One sister even hosts a family game night as our mother and grandmother used to. We try to spend time together every chance we get. My four sisters and I celebrate *Sister Weekend* several times a year, getting away and spending time enjoying each other's company and reminiscing about family memories. It is something my mother and her sisters used to enjoy as well.

I miss her. The older I get, the more I realize the legacy and lessons my mother left for her children were significant and inspiring. They have helped shape my destiny and purpose. It is important to me and my family that we continue to share these lessons. We want the love and dedication Eva showed in her lifetime to continue to reach out and touch others. She would have liked it that way.

Holly Strickland

Holly Strickland is Mother to five adult children – Crystal, Cicely, Clinton, Christopher and Caitlyn – who have learned to make good choices, give back to the community and take care of family!

*Mother Eva and my father
Holly Strickland*

*Mom had her faults ...
But because of these faults
I am Me*

"Put a Band-Aid on it" and other lessons learned from my mother

My mother was what one might call a 'Southern Belle.' Born Mary Elizabeth Gillis in 1923, she grew up in South Georgia and then made her way as far north as Atlanta. She met my Libyan father, Suleiman Dahan, in Atlanta and married him soon after in 1957 in London, and then moved with him to Tripoli, Libya. My mother was not a woman of her time. Who moved to Tripoli back in 1957? There was barely good long distance service, never mind the Internet!

So, as a daring woman, one might imagine Elizabeth was an awesome mother. There were many things about her that were awesome and fun and adventurous. Unfortunately, my mother was an alcoholic, and back in the day, this was not something people talked about or staged interventions for. It was just a fact of life, and it was often very difficult for those living with her. However, I will not dwell on the negative. Instead, I celebrate the many things I learned from her. I consider myself a strong, independent woman who is willing to fight the long, hard fight to gain what I need in life and to ensure my children get what they require and deserve. Much of that will and perseverance came directly from my mother's influence.

My mother died from liver cancer in 1989. She has not been part of my life for decades; yet, there is hardly a day that goes by that I don't think of a story she told me, or about something she pointed out to me about child-rearing, cooking, reading, studying, people, family, you name it. Her voice is still with me because she was an essential part of my life, and she was so animated in her story-telling back then. She loved to talk at length about her family, her childhood in Georgia, her college years, how she and her family managed during the Great Depression and World War II, her two brothers and one cousin who all went off to war, and more. She also told many interesting tales about her life with my father in Tripoli. From her I gained insight into my Libyan heritage.

My mother told great stories. She talked about all the letters she wrote home to family, and the difficulty of making long distance calls because the operators only spoke Arabic and no English. Her stories were entertaining, but also enlightening. I learned a lot about the American and Libyan sides of my family through them.

My mother's first job in the US after graduating from college was as an English teacher, and she was extremely well-read. But after a few years of teaching, she returned to university and earned her master's degree in library science. Books were her world, and I never saw her without one. No matter what she was involved with, a book was nearby. My father's degree was in journalism, but he worked for the Libyan government when my parents met in Atlanta. Both of them were voracious readers, and that definitely imprinted upon me and my siblings. We are rarely without a book, and we would often and still do discuss what we are reading and what we should read next.

I am glad I love to read. I like telling stories too. I don't feel I do justice to stories as she did, but I try to continue the tradition with my own sons. I tell them about their grandparents, because they never met either of them. Both my parents died long before I got married. It is up to me to ensure they have stories about Grandma Elizabeth and Grandpa Suleiman to connect to our past. Just as my mother told me stories about her life growing up, I tell my boys about my life growing up in Libya. I developed the need to keep stories of the family alive, and for that I am grateful to my mother.

From Mother, I also learned to be tough and non-emotional in the face of broken bones, bloody gashes, and other revolting ailments. I have many friends who tell me how they call for help whenever their children are injured. Even my sons' father could never handle any of the medical emergencies I have dealt with. But from Mother I developed the attitude that any bone that might be broken could benefit from some aspirin, a cold compress, or perhaps a soak in a warm tub.

When I was young, she would often treat major injuries, which even left one of us with spewing blood, with rubbing alcohol and a Band-Aid. I have taken a more centered approach to injuries. I take my boys to the ER when needed and don't just assume a bone is not broken. However, thanks to Mother, I don't panic when the blood won't stop flowing, and I don't stress over bones that might be fractured.

When my sister gashed her leg in a bike accident long ago, my mother applied Band-Aids that kept soaking through. My brother, who had his fair share of stitches, pointed out that my sister would require stitches for that accident. When I fell off a horse and hit a fence, Mother gave me some aspirin and told me to take a hot bath. After an x-ray, which my father took me for, mind you, we discovered I had two fractured vertebrae. We laugh now as adults about Mother and her "cures," but my siblings and I are quite happy to be "tough," and there are no worries about hypochondriacs here.

From my mother I also learned to be independent. Some of that was unintentional on her part, since her needed guidance was often missing, but she did allow me to take care of things myself before asking for help. I sometimes worry now that I don't ask for help when I need it, and I know that is not ideal, but I also am happy I am not needy and am quite content to do things on my own.

Being independent allowed me to adjust to the many moves my family made in the late 1970s. When I was 14, the Libyan political situation forced us to leave the only home I ever knew, Libya, for the safe haven of Rome, Italy. Mother never made us feel as though leaving our country was a scary or threatening issue. Instead, with her casual demeanor, she started up a new home in Rome. So, despite being surrounded by everything new, I managed. I learned to take public transportation, and I even got a small motor bike I rode around on the main roads. When we moved to Morocco just two years later, my parents ended up on a small farm outside Rabat, while I went to a boarding school in Tangier. I soon graduated and left for the US to begin university in Washington, DC. Thanks to the self-sufficiency I learned from Mother, this move was also smooth.

I am not saying it was easy, but I am thankful to Mother for pushing me to be independent, ensuring that I never sat around feeling bad for the way our lives turned out after leaving Libya, and for showing me my education came first. Her regular letters to me in her beautiful script kept her stories of Moroccan life alive for me while I was far away at college. My love of writing surely comes from my mother's insistence on keeping in touch and sharing our lives through the written word.

And finally, from Mother I learned to persevere, to never assume I had lost an opportunity to pursue my dream, even if that dream may be put on hold for years. My PhD is an example. I never gave up; I wanted that final degree and no matter what got in the way, I kept at it and earned my PhD. There are so many roadblocks that can stand in our way if we allow them to. I often feel I have had more than my share of roadblocks in life, but I know others who have faced even more hardships than I. Whenever life didn't go my way, I just learned to roll with it and keep going, because that is how Mother did it.

Life, very often, is not easy. Mother knew that, and so do I. Although my mother had a fairly prosperous life married to my father, the years living in exile in Italy and Morocco took a financial toll. Nonetheless, no matter how rough it got, Mother never gave up, from the grand days of Tripoli in the late 1950s until the revolution of 1969. The move to Italy in 1976 was a big change, but she managed it. She kept us all going, never indicating we were in any danger from the Libyan government, or that we might run out of money, lessons we learned as adults.

She carried on with life. Even after we had to leave Rome, due to an incident involving men in masks, guns, and chaos in our own home, thanks to Gadhafi and the Libyan government, she soldiered on. We moved to Morocco, and she ended up living on a farm in the middle of nowhere, with no phone, and electricity supplied by a generator only at night. She didn't make a fuss; she sent her children off to different countries to continue our educations, and she stayed there with my father. Mother did not particularly like nature or animals, but she managed.

I learned many lessons from Mother: to be strong in the face of adversity, to be tough when you are scared, to show the world life is being managed, even as it crumbles around you. Mother showed me strength, perseverance in the face of adversity, and how to be brave, push onward, and to limit feelings of helplessness and fear. Mother never conquered her own alcoholism, but on a good day, she was awesome, strong, and a helpful guide for how to get on with life.

When my father died under mysterious circumstances, my mother was left alone. It was a horrific time for her and for all of us. My father was only 58-years-old. He had so much ahead of him, but his life was cut short like many other Libyan exiles of that time at the hands Gadhafi's cruelty. Mother always appeared so strong during the extremely scary and confusing days following my father's death. She acted brave, put on a good front, and my brother, sister, and I all assumed she was holding it all together.

Not until nearly thirty years later, when I was writing a book about my mother, did I unearth some letters she had written to one of my American cousins during that time. What I discovered in those letters broke my heart. Mother had written during those dark days in Morocco following my father's death that she felt like screaming and crying, but she wanted to be "strong for the children." Those words made me so sad. We were not children at that time; I was 19 and my brother and sister were older than I. But being the strong Southern woman, Mother had determined that her children would not see her sorrow, because it was her job to keep us going. That notion makes me depressed even today, knowing she held back her own pain and sorrow for us.

In the end, in addition to the many things I learned from my mother, I also know some things she did will never be a part of my own children's lives. Having lived with a mother who was great on a good day but who often left us lonely, I have vowed never to allow my two boys to feel that way. I may not be a perfect mother, but I am never absent. I pick them up when I promise to, and am available to them whenever we are home. I do my best to ensure they feel safe, protected, and noticed at all times.

When I look back at life with Mother, I focus on the good times: the positive impact she had on me, her love of books and family, her ability to manage stressful and confusing situations, her wonderful stories, and her eccentricities. I remember those good times for my sons. I miss her today as much as I did when I lost her back in 1989.

Mothers come in a vast array of types, but one thing most of us know is that we loved them when they were with us, and we continue to love them in their absence, because they taught us, loved us, and shaped the people who we are today.

Laila Suleiman Dahan, Ph.D.

Laila S. Dahan is an independent researcher and teacher, who recently relocated to California from the United Arab Emirates, where she taught composition at the American University of Sharjah. She holds MAs in political science and TESOL and a PhD in language education. She publishes in a wide range of fields, most recently "One boy's journey: Living with autism in the UAE" in the Journal of Psychology and Behavioral Science *(2015), and two chapters coming out in 2017: "Reflections on the hijab: Choice or obligation?" in the anthology* Mirror on the veil: A collection of personal essays on hijab and veiling *and "The age of global English: Language use and identity construction in the United Arab Emirates" in the edited volume* Applied linguistics in the Middle East and North Africa. *She also published* Keep your feet hidden: A southern belle on the shores of Tripoli, *a memoir about her mother.*

No forth

It was you
who taught me
the word: *No*.

When it came to boys
I was a retard
about the *No* thing.

A yes-girl in Nowheresville,
a *No*-virgin at seventeen.
Even my mother failed at *No*.

You can't take No
for an answer, can you?
she accused. Regularly.

Locked me in my room
for a summer month once.
Grounded. Bummer.

I'd fall asleep to the squeaky
wheel of Chopin the Hamster,
fellow creature in a cage.

However, no maternally-
induced *No* stopped me,
her *No* lesson,

her *No* of waning power.
But your *No*!
Your *No* étude,

your practiced measures
of *No*, always

in a minor key,

a long opus of *No*s.
Then *the No*.
The final *No*.

At least now I know why.

Karla Linn Merrifield

Grandma taught her to love life
Sueann Wells

Lesson

Near the end of June in the heat that's steamy and heavy with the perfume of earth and grass and trees, tent worms are busy - spinning, eating, birthing within their gauze-gray rooms. The tree branches in our back yard pull down in the weight of their making. The tents look like paper lanterns in need of lights.

The worms disturb my mother. She can hear their mandibulars chewing on tender green leaves. She knows she has to do something to save her trees. She thinks fire is a solution, and calls me, a willing fourteen-year-old, to help her fashion newspaper torches on opened wire coat hangers.

As we do this, she explains: "We'll take the yellow step stool out back and place it under the branches, then you climb up the step stool and stand on the seat. I'll light the torch and pass it to you. You stick the fire into the tents and that will be that, right?" I go along with my mother's plan, not imagining anything could go wrong. She speaks with such authority on how to do things I don't question her.

When I'm standing up on the stool's seat, she passes the flaming torch to me. I raise it up over my head into the branches, and suddenly it starts to break apart in red hot clumps, landing on my outstretched forearms. The smell of singed hair rank, the heat sharp as pinpricks, I start flailing and howling. My mother stands below transfixed. She can't move or talk. I jump down, torch in hand, landing on the grass. Ashes fall everywhere.

I look up at my mother looking at me, and hold out my arm. "I'm burned. This is really stupid. I trusted you." My mother looks me over carefully and says I'll be all right, but adds, "Don't trust anyone, not even your mother."

M.J. Iuppa

M.J. Iuppa first published "Lesson" in Tiny Lights (online), in Eating the Pure Light: Homage to Thomas McGrath, *edited by John Bradley, and later in* Between Worlds *(Foothills Publishing, 2013).*

Moms are human, too

When I was growing up, there were many times when I disagreed with my mother's words and actions. As a teenager, disagreement was properly verbalized (improper speech meant a swat on the face). I can still remember my mother's response: "If you think another way is better, just do it differently with your own children."

I look back now and smile. Yes, I have done some things differently. However, my mother taught me the important things in life, such as:

Work hard

Go to church

You are never alone

Stand up for what is right

Have endurance – keep trying

Change a bad system from within

Talk positively or close your mouth

Do your best and that is good enough

Only make promises you intend to keep

Pray regularly – it will get you through rough times

Live within your means and you will have the means to live

Give 10% back to God - He will make the remaining 90% cover your needs

And, the hardest lesson of all for me as a parent: *We all make mistakes.*

A good example of my mother making a mistake: A box came for my mother one December, while she was at work. No one else was home, so I opened the top of the humungous thing. Inside was a beautiful metal pole desk, with a "V" shelf for books, a writing shelf, and a smaller shelf underneath to keep supplies. I loved it and hoped it was for me, but inside my heart I knew better. My older brother was always the favored one. I was the third child and frequently felt like I just received "leftovers." Carefully, I retaped the box and nothing more was said about it.

On Christmas morning, I beamed! There was that great big box on MY chair! When I opened it and squealed, I heard my mother say to my brother, "That was going to be yours, but you opened the box. Therefore, you don't get it." My brother tried to argue, but she wouldn't listen. I hadn't quite learned that silence at the wrong time was as bad as lying outright, so I never offered the truth.

Did I learn anything positive from that? Yes, actually I did. Although I admit I enjoyed that one really good gift for many years, I learned that even mothers make mistakes.

So, as a mother, I tried to make sure I asked the right questions. I also tried to make sure that favoritism had no place in my home. My children can cite examples of when I managed to break my own rules, but at least I tried. (Both children think the other one was my favorite).

For the longest time, I worried about my reaction to a child who produced a $10 bill for a purchase, even though we didn't give allowances. I immediately thought it was stolen, so I took it away and put it in my purse. Then I worried it taught the wrong lesson. Did I really teach that stealing was wrong? Or did I teach that a person could scrimp and save and then have the money grabbed away? For years I worried about that one incident. Recently, my adult child admitted the money had been taken from a stash I kept for incidental expenses like extra milk and bread. So I didn't take away money that didn't belong to me!

Now, though, hindsight shows that a decision not to give allowances might have caused this problem. We wanted the children to know that household chores were merely part of living as a family, not something they get paid to do. Yet, we lived out in the country where neighbors were "few and far between." There really wasn't any way for my children to earn money. Therefore, once released from the self-imposed guilt of taking back that $10 bill, guilt still haunted me about the no-allowance rule.

This is just one of many times when I have doubted my past actions and abilities as a mother. I have lost sleep even years later over some of my actions. At those times, I rehash the circumstances and try to imagine what would have happened if I had done or said something else. To get out of the funk, I remember that my mother made mistakes, too.

I also realized something my own mother had tried to teach me: As long as a mother's decisions are made with love, wanting to teach a positive life lesson, everything will work out okay. The children will survive and thrive.

Thank you, Mom, for teaching me that mothers are human, too!

Karen Hockenberry

Nadine General

Contributors' Index

Bailey, Ron 19, 23, 24, 38

Banser, Heidi 69

Baruch, Susan 34

Campbell, Emery 13

Dahan, Laila Suleiman 74

General, Nadine 86

Gleason, Krista 28

Green, Christine 88

Hockenberry, Karen ..... cover photo, 30, 39, 48, 57, 83

Hotaling, Lisa Carley 88

Iuppa, M.J. 82

Merrifield, Karla Linn 80

Sparks, Jerri Lynn 8, 15, 51

Strickland, Holly 70

Tilley, Cyndalynn 20

Vogt, Sue 64

Vukosic, Katelynn 26

Vukosic, Kay 26

Wells, Aaron 42

Wells, Kayla 41

Wells, Sueann 10, 43

My Mother Taught Me examines motherhood in all its complexities and nuances. In this delightful volume of poetry and prose you can find mothers who were present and mothers who were absent, mothers who laughed every day and mothers who cried more often than not, mothers who raised their children all on their own and mothers who had a partner by their side. The pages are alive with the diverse mothers who gave each contributor their advice, love, and life-lessons. A great gift for the new mother or for Mother's Day, *My Mother Taught Me*, is a lovely tribute to the women who raised us.

~ Christine Green, Literary Arts Columnist, Democrat and Chronicle

As our nation struggles to find its way in an increasingly divided political and cultural climate, perhaps the healing of our country doesn't begin with simply listening to those with whom we disagree or trying to understand different points of view. We all know how good this sounds in theory and just how difficult it is in practice. Instead, it is my growing belief that it is mothers who can bring us together. As mothers, we are united in our wish for the best for our kids, for being good examples, for pinning our hopes on a future that offers opportunities for happiness and peace.

Sueann Wells has brought together a collection of narratives, in prose, poetry, and photography that reminds us of the maternal thread that both tethered us to this earth when we were born and cut us loose into an uncertain adulthood. In *My Mother Taught Me*, Wells deftly weaves together disparate strands to create a cohesive narrative made all the stronger and all the richer for its diversity.

Anthologies that both venerate and interrogate the maternal experience serve to bring us closer together. Sueann Wells has not only bound us together through powerful maternal narratives; she has reminded us that perhaps our best hope for an empowered future rests with an appreciation that for some, a walk in the woods may open up even the most closed among us, and for others, the refusal to settle for an unripe melon may just be the start of finding one's conviction.

~ Lisa Carley Hotaling, Editor, The Narrow Pass